Funny
Old Sayings

Allana Worthington

BALBOA.
PRESS
A DIVISION OF HAY HOUSE

Balboa Press books may be ordered through booksellers or by contacting:

Balboa Press
A Division of Hay House
1663 Liberty Drive
Bloomington, IN 47403
www.balboapress.com.au
1 (877) 407-4847

Print information available on the last page.

ISBN: 978-1-5043-0570-9 (sc)
ISBN: 978-1-5043-0571-6 (e)

Balboa Press rev. date: 12/19/2016

It's nice to be important but more important to be nice.

No good throwing the baby out with the bathwater.

Grizzling about it won't get you anywhere.

Life's a joke, and then you croak.

The tables will turn on him.

Less hurry, more haste.

Neat as a pin.

Don't put all your eggs in one basket.

No need to get shirty.

A wigwam for a goose's bridle.

Sling your hook.

Wouldn't be dead for quid's.

Love many, trust few, and always
paddle your own canoe.

A few too many under the belt.

Up in old Annie's room behind the clock.

Top of the morning to you.

A tidy little sum.

Great minds think alike.

Just a little snippet.

Crooked as a dog's hind leg.

Time heals all wounds and wounds all heels.

Life's a bitch, and then you die.

On the last lap.

Done and dusted.

Taken for a ride.

A problem shared is a problem halved.

A nine-day wonder.

Off your own bat.

That takes the biscuit.

Couldn't lay straight in bed.

She'll steal the show.

Top of the heap.

Build a bridge, and get over it.

A few skeletons in the closet.

You're getting up my nose.

To run with the fox and chase with the hounds.

Drop a size before the mince pies.

The pennies just dropped.

In the running.

Having a brainwave.

Make a beeline for the door.

It's all gone up in smoke.

I must crack on.

2y'sur, 2y'sub, icur 2y's4 me.

Make hay while the sun shines.

Quick off the mark.

Not a bad pair of pins.

You rat fink.

Not much of a track record.

As mad as a hatter.

While the cat's away, the mice will play.

Curiosity killed the cat.

Too good to be true.

Holy terror.

Got his pound of flesh.

Mind your own beeswax.

She's a fly in the ointment.

That's got him stumped.

Waste not; want not.

Nothing but a boil on the arse of society.

Over the moon.

He's hell-bent on it.

He's off his bloody trolley.

A few kangaroos short in the top paddock.

They are posh.

As funny as a play.

Hat trick.

Three sheets to the wind.

Pot calling the kettle black.

He's under the thumb.

She's over the hill.

He's as bent as.

Just going to spend a penny.

Sailing close to the wind.

One fell swoop.

Bit of a loose cannon.

To gild the lily.

Bugger you, Jack. I'm all right.

Off your dial.

Like a pimple on a pumpkin.

That's a bit over the top.

A face as long, as a fiddle.

On your bike.

Telling porky pies.

A real snake in the grass.

That'll throw him off the scent.

Eat shit, and die.

Running out of juice.

I could have crawled under a threepenny bit.

Not much chop.

Couldn't shit in the ocean without getting caught.

It'll be a walk in the park.

Takes one to know one.

Fading away to a shadow.

Cat on hot bricks.

Pipped at the post.

I can't take a trick.

You have painted yourself into a corner.

It's curtains for him.

Keep me in the loop.

Top billing.

On top of the world.

Getting on my nerves.

Shit a brick.

Once bitten, twice shy.

Pay through the nose.

Pigs might fly.

Out on a limb.

Show a leg.

A bird in the hand is worth two in the bush.

To the manner born.

Wake up and smell the roses.

It was like lying on a bed of nails.

Wardrobe drinker.

Going like a bat out of hell.

You're driving me crazy.

Do you think that's fair play?

Bit of a dark horse.

Sitting on your derrière.

Spare the rod; spoil the child.

That's bull dust.

That's not cricket.

Digging your own grave.

Believe none of what you hear and
only half of what you see.

You can choose your friends, but you
can't choose your family.

Built like a brick shithouse.

Blood's thicker than water.

Better the devil you know than the one you don't.

Like a bull at a gate.

By and large.

Swallow the bait.

Ten-ton Tessie.

If it were raining sausages, I'd grab a turd.

Wouldn't give him the steam off my shit.

The quiet mouse gets the cheese.

Leave well enough alone.

Keep your trap shut.

I could eat the crotch out of a low-flying duck.

She's a head-turner.

Being led up the garden path.

It was no walk in the park.

Butter wouldn't melt in your mouth.

Just about petered out.

The old ball and chain.

It means squat to me.

I certainly had him pegged.

There is going to be the devil to pay when they find out.

Don't try buttering me up.

Didn't sleep a wink.

Wet my whistle.

That was out of left field.

Bottoms up.

There's no fool like an old fool.

That took the wind out of his sails.

Tit for tat.

A watched pot never boils.

That was a close shave.

Better to be safe than sorry.

She is worth her weight in gold.

By jingoes.

I'm bushed.

Old fancy pants.

Tender loving care.

That was out of the blue.

Old bossy boots.

To start from scratch.

Like lambs to the slaughter.

Stick it up your clacker.

Sugar and spice and all things nice.

In for a penny, in for a pound.

That'll warm the cockles of your heart.

I'm gobsmacked.

Winning by a nose.

Money burns a hole in your pocket.

Speak of the devil.

Too little, too late.

Broad in the beam.

Better get your skates on.

Here's looking at you, kid.

Just a nosy so-and-so.

Sent to Coventry.

It's Greek to me.

Shape up, or ship out.

Mud sticks.

Gone like a Bondi tram.

Down in the dumps.

As clear as the nose on your face.

Turn the other cheek.

Thumbs up.

What the Sam Hill?

Going for a song.

Life in the fast lane.

Chuck a wobbly.

There's method in his madness.

Toe the line.

If you're on a good thing, stick to it.

You're a boof head.

Brighten up your ideas.

You're a silly Billy.

Save the best till last.

Silly as a rabbit.

He runs a tight ship.

Throw a tanty.

Stuck up so-and-so.

Got you hook, line, and sinker.

As green as grass.

A charmed life.

Win hands down.

Bleeding like a stuck pig.

Give someone the cold shoulder.

Keeping up with the Joneses.

That'll open the floodgates.

On Queer Street.

Show him the ropes.

That's let the cat out of the bag.

The grass is always greener on the
other side of the fence.

Stick it up your derrière.

You're a silly duffer.

Cheers, big ears.

Sticks and stones may break my bones,
but names will never hurt me.

It's bigger than Ben-Hur.

Grin and bear it.

Your mums on the warpath.

That's mind-boggling.

You're living in dreamland.

Gone up in a puff of smoke.

On a slow boat to China.

Dog breath.

As quick as a wink.

You've created havoc.

That'll put a smile on his dial.

Get down to the nitty-gritty.

Cheeky chops.

Just kidding around.

Not up to scratch.

If you play your cards right.

That is madness.

I did a double take.

Little poppet.

He's just hit the wall.

Old grizzle guts.

Jockeying for a position.

Stop your bellyaching.

He's a bit of a dirt bag.

Blaze a trail.

As cheap as chips.

Windy britches.

As mad as a wet hen.

Cut your cloth to suit your needs.

Put a gobstopper in it.

It's like pushing shit uphill with a stick.

Never a dull moment.

Can't go the distance.

Just in the nick of time.

You're not towing the line.

Don't quote me.

Done like a dinner.

Don't bust your boiler.

Keep your hair on.

Mouth like a gutter trap.

Jumping the gun.

Hallmark of quality.

Got a bee in her bonnet.

Put your money where your mouth is.

Straight from the horse's mouth.

Dunny roll.

Penny for your thoughts.

Pull some strings.

You've upset the old apple cart.

Let him off the hook.

I've got other fish to fry.

That's a turn up for the books.

Not short of a quid.

Doubting Thomas.

You hit the nail on the head.

In the limelight.

Keep your nose out of it.

Running like a cat on a hot tin roof.

They're head to head.

Loose lips sink ships.

You've burnt your bridges now.

Put your best foot forward.

Kick up your heels.

I was taken aback.

Flat out like a lizard drinking.

All in good time.

Keep your nose clean.

My hair is standing on end like a birch broom in a fit.

Going to hit the hay.

Your hair looks like you've crawled
through a bush backwards.

The bigger they are, the harder they fall.

Shit sticks to a blanket.

Birds of a feather flock together.

Its touch and go.

Beauty is only skin deep.

Have you got ants in your pants?

In two shakes of a lamb's tail.

Beauty is in the eye of the beholder.

That should keep the wolves from the door.

Dinky-di Aussie.

Good riddance to bad rubbish.

Not in the running.

Bit cloak and dagger.

Where is it? On the corner of the round table!

Just the duck's guts.

The less said, the better.

He's a busy little beaver.

Let's bury the hatchet.

I'll have a small morsel.

Bob's your uncle; Fanny's your aunt.

Mrs. Kerfoops. (A term used when someone
was not sure of the person's name.)

Heavy going.

Somewhere up whoop-whoop.

Bit long in the tooth.

She's no spring chicken.

Lady muck.

It's Rafferty's rules around here.

For fun and fancy to please old Nancy.

Sweet Larry Dooley.

I'm pipped off.

We don't stand on ceremony here.

Drawn a blank.

Old Joe blow.

Old Reg grundies. (A man's undies.)

Keep things on an even keel.

In like Flynn.

Pulling his strings.

Across the board.

You've got Buckley's and none.

Sweet Fanny Adams.

Doesn't know whether he's Arthur or Martha.

Going flat chat.

Just shrapnel to them.

Even blind Freddie could see that.

Suffering the Edgar Britt's and Farmer Giles.

It sent shivers up my spine.

He's dragging his bum around.

Don't bang on about it.

Wouldn't work in an iron lung.

Passing the buck.

Hooley Dooley.

Never say never.

Just in case I fall off the perch.

In your dreams.

As dead as a doornail.

Jimmy woodsier.

Up shit creek without a paddle.

Don't dilly dally.

She's a walk over.

I can read you like an open book.

The die is cast.

Dancing like a cat on a hot tin roof.

Don't worry; be happy.

Get a rise out of her.

It hurts like billy-o.

He can go to buggery.

House devil, street angel.

No good shutting the stable door,
after the horse has bolted.

Stop pussy footing around.

Tell it like it is.

We're all in the same boat.

We all have our cross to bear.

I was gob smacked.

He's like a bull in a china shop.

Dressed like a fashion plate.

Has the cat got your tongue?

Blazing a trail.

Running off at the mouth.

To look a gift horse in the mouth.

Monkey see, monkey do.

Come on, shake a leg.

Won by a whisker.

Time's a great healer.

Only time will tell.

Stealing the show.

Come on, cough it up.

Spit it out, for goodness' sake.

Got to face the music.

As different as chalk and cheese.

Perched up there like Jackie.

Backed the wrong horse.

Good for a laugh.

Let's see if it stands the test of time.

It'll all come out in the wash.

He took it like a trooper.

He hasn't got a kind bone in his body.

They hung him out to dry.

Don't try and whitewash it.

Fox smells its own scent first.

It's just not cricket.

Come up smelling like roses.

On the rocks.

Clean up your act.

No strings attached.

Silly old sod.

What a mamby pamby. (Lacking character or substance.)

Gone past his use-by date.

On his last legs.

Darn old britches.

He's got shit on the liver.

A face like thunder.

Between the devil and the deep blue sea.

We'll have to make ends meet.

There's more than one way to skin a cat.

It was the last straw that broke the camel's back.

I'll give her an earful.

All brawn and no brains.

Born with a silver spoon in her mouth.

She's a cracker, isn't she?

Bit of a tear jerker.

Sweet mother of mine.

The old cheese.

He's past it.

Keep a lid on it.

See you later, alligator.

In a while, crocodile.

After lunch, honey bunch.

I've pulled the plug on that one.

I'll drink to that.

All at sixes and sevens.

Stop your tattling.

Put two and two together.

Means to an end.

As bright as a button.

Needle in a haystack.

What a Godsend.

Howdy rowdy.

Live for today.

Making small talk.

Pie in the sky idea.

Screaming like a stuck pig.

It's as clear as mud.

Be a good sport.

Make a fresh start.

Dirty old sod.

Clean as a whistle.

A real diehard.

He's a real character.

Going to the loo.

Like a pig in a poke.

You're a bright spark.

Horses for courses.

He was chucking boondies.

Practice makes perfect.

Pot of gold at the end of the rainbow.

Drunk as a skunk.

It's like Chinese torture.

Pissed as a cricket.

Get off your high horse.

A right so-and-so.

Out of the mouths of babes.

Get a grip.

Party like there is no tomorrow.

Drinks like a fish.

As mad as a rabbit.

Sink the boots in, why don't you?

Don't keep gabbing on.

Silly as a hare.

I smell a rat.

Cooped up like chickens.

Going off like a firecracker.

Better late than never.

It's all in a day's work.

Worked my fingers to the bone.

Swaying in the breeze.

Don't tittle tat.

Sucked in, jumped on, and spat at.

Quit horsing around.

Too many cooks spoil the broth.

Let's have a sneak peek.

Pain in my pinny.

Get off your bandbox.

Gently Bentley.

Up to his neck in it.

Those kids have been pushed from pillar to post.

There's life in the old dog yet.

A stitch in time saves nine.

Foul play.

Bit of a loser.

Wouldn't say shit for a shilling.

Not worth two bob.

A real bright idea.

A right piece of work.

Look at old twinkle toes.

Just going to get forty winks.

Away with the fairies.

Lay down with dogs, and you'll get fleas.

You've made my day.

You live and learn.

You silly sausage.

Going like a Bondi tram.

First come, first served.

Like laying on a bed of nails.

Cheap at half the price.

It's raining cats and dogs, and
there's poodles on the road.

I'll box your ears.

Stick it where the sun don't shine.

He's sleeping like a baby.

Skinny Minnie.

Back-stabbing bitch.

There's proof in the pudding.

Let's hit the frog and toad.

He's gone to the dogs.

She's got her claws into him.

It had me on the edge of my seat.

No pain, no gain.

Live and let live.

I'll wring your neck.

Come off the grass.

Party animal.

He's got the devil in him.

Little Dennis the menace.

It's as plain as the nose on your face.

They're coming neck and neck.

You're giving me the tom tits.

Let's not split hairs.

Baby steps first.

Don't bite the hand that feeds you.

Learning the tricks of the trade.

Once seen never forgotten.

Stepping on his toes.

Cut it out.

That's his bread and butter.

It's a storm in a teacup.

That's how the land lies.

Luck of the draw.

In a bit of a tight spot.

It's all coming up roses.

Full as a po.

He's taken the bait.

Hard yakka.

Jump in feet first.

Shut your claptrap.

Son of a bitch.

Wrap your chops around that.

That tickled your fancy.

Don't rock the boat.

Bit of an agony aunt.

Can't see the forest for the tree's.

Souped-up car.

Real old banger.

Down the hatch.

One step at a time.

Worth a quid or two.

Real knuckleduster.

We're just going around in circles.

Old dizzy Lizzy.

Went through me like a packet of salts.

Gives me the heebie-jeebies.

Tracky daks.

I'll have his guts for garters.

He wouldn't have two bob to rub together.

Everyone has a cross to bare.

Bob a job.

I'm tickled pink about that.

Gone in the twinkle of an eye.

Top of the day to you.

People who live in glass houses shouldn't throw stones.

You've made your bed; now lie in it.

Least said, soonest mended.

You're off the hook.

He has two left feet.

Happy hunting ground.

As black as the ace of spades.

Tried and true.

He's on the dunny.

You're pushing your luck.

She's got a good set of pegs.

Fair dinkum mate.

Crikey Moses.

What the heck is that?

Took to it like a duck to water.

Got everything but the kitchen sink.

He's pushing up daisies.

Like a bolt out of the blue.

It's as plain as day.

Hair past a freckle.

As cold as ice.

Full as a goog.

You're punching above your weight.

Running out of steam.

Googy eggs for breaky.

Hat full of monkeys.

I've run out of steam.

I'll be a monkey's uncle.

Jumping jackass.

The shape of things to come.

You'll have to fend for yourself.

Wouldn't spit on him, if he was on fire.

For Pete's sake.

Well, I'll be.

The patience of a saint.

You'd drive a man to drink.

Thick as a brick.

I'm going there and back to see how far it is.

As long, as a piece of string. (As a child when asking how long is it?)

For crying out loud.

He's on the thunder box.

Looking down her nose.

Had a change of heart.

Looks like a sack of spuds.

Have you had your two bobs' worth?

Home, James, and don't spare the horses.

Hanging around like a bad smell.

Steer clear of him.

Put that in your pipe and smoke it.

Gentle giant.

That's a cheap line, if I've heard one.

A bit worse for wear.

I'll tear him apart.

You're cracking me up.

It's a dog's life.

Hang in there.

In the pink.

Out by the black stump.

We'd better skedaddle out of here.

Trying to get my head around it.

I'll need to do a bit of grovelling.

You're giving me the willies.

Stone the flaming crows.

Only a stone's throw away.

Stop tiptoeing around it.

Stop dilly-dallying.

You can hear the cogs turning.

Out behind the black stump.

Got your penny's worth.

Get over yourself.

Hit me like a kick in the guts.

Like a fish out of water.

You flaming galah.

New set of wheels.

Like a pack of wolves.

She's got a great set of pins.

Stubby short of a carton.

A face like a half-eaten pastie.

Up to pussies' bow.

Old wives' tale.

Betwixt and between.

Hit the deck.

Go jump in the lake.

Don't let the sods get you down.

He's in fine form.

God gave me broad shoulders.

Stick to your guns.

I didn't come down in the last shower.

Avoid him like the plague.

Knock your socks off.

He's got the collywobbles.

Stack high in transit (SHIT: Manure on boats).

Gentlemen only; ladies forbidden (GOLF).

Like a streak of pump water.

I'll have to save your bacon.

Coming by pigeon post.

Just idle chit-chat.

Having a chin wag.

I've got a dodgy ticker.

Shot that one out of the water.

You beat me to the punch.

Look me in the eye.

He's got a good right hook.

A bit of Argy Bargy.

Budgie smugglers.

As dry as a wooden god.

Full of beans.

Cat burglar.

Oh, my giddy aunt.

Pennies from heaven.

Miss goody two shoes.

Oldie but a Goldie.

Better than a poke in the eye with a stick.

Live in hope; die in vain.

Black sheep of the family.

No rest for the wicked.

That's a load of codswallop.

Struck pay dirt.

Go take a flying leap.

He's straight down the line.

Cooked your goose, for sure.

There's no smoke without fire.

All you'll get is the dregs from the bottom of the barrel.

Hop to it, girl.

Up to dolly's wax.

It's all a pipe dream.

A barrel of laughs.

Life's not all beer and skittles.

He is so chuffed.

Pub grub.

Don't go jumping the gun.

Happy as two peas in a pod.

No point buying the welcome mat before the house.

Party pooper.

Penny pincher.

I hate to burst your bubble.

That ruffled his feathers.

I'm left to pick up the pieces.

We've got a fox in the henhouse.

Chief cook and bottle-washer.

As free as a bird.

You're a knucklehead.

The old ticker's playing up.

Jack of all trades, master of none.

Like a slap in the face with a wet fish.

Went like clockwork.

Smack you in the kiss-a-roo.

The shoes on the other foot now.

Feathering his own nest.

Stood the test of time.

He's as silly as a wheel.

Bit of a scatterbrain.

Stick a few homeward bounders in it.

Don't bottle things up.

You can't make a silk purse out of a sow's ear.

Stop your tomfooling around.

More hands make light work.

Brand-spanking-new.

Saved by the bell.

Dressed to kill.

Just a twinkle in your dad's eye.

Best bib and tucker.

Love you to bits.

Shut your trap.

Going to see a man about a dog.

Chock-a-block.

Better top up the juice.

Where there's smoke, there's fire.

Stick that in your pipe and smoke it.

Your way or the highway.

You're as weak as water.

Blow me down.

As silly as a cut snake.

Well, tickle me pink.

You're as light as a feather.

Laughing my head off.

Give it your best shot.

Bit of a tight squeeze.

What's that face for?

Shut your gob.

Put pen to paper.

Bit of a cheapskate.

They're well heeled.

My achy-breaky bones.

What a lot of hullabaloo.

Stop you're kicking off.

That's a shot in the dark.

As black as soot.

Bit of a tall order.

I couldn't give a tinker's cuss.

Bit of a stick in the mud.

You can thank your lucky stars for that.

That's between you, me, and the gatepost fence.

It made my blood boil.

Long pockets, short arms.

See a penny, pick it up; then all
day, you'll have good luck.

We found the baby in the cabbage patch.

Out of sight, out of mind.

What a lot of bunkum.

Like a red rag to a bull.

A rolling stone gathers no moss.

You're a sight, for sore eyes.

As proud as, a peacock.

Just a stone's throw from here.

Strike me dead.

Bit of a blood-sucking leech, that one.

What doesn't kill you makes you stronger.

Rough as guts.

A wolf in sheep's clothing.

I haven't slept a wink.

As safe as, houses.

Out of sorts.

A word in your shell-like.

What a shemozzle.

What's good for the goose is good for the gander.

He's legging it.

Act the giddy goat.

Egg all over my face.

As fit, as a fiddle.

I'll swing for him.

As sound, as a bell.

One for the road.

Age before beauty.

Not for all the tea in China.

All fingers and thumbs.

If the cap fits.

All that glitters, is not gold.

You take care of the pennies, and the pounds will take care of themselves.

Hold that thought.

An eye for an eye, and a tooth for a tooth.

As brown as a berry.

Like chalk and cheese.

Cool as a cucumber.

They are the talk of the town.

The apple of my eye.

If it ain't broke, don't fix it.

He's a jammy bugger.

As happy as a sand boy.

He's as keen as mustard.

One hit wonder.

Whoops a daisy.

Strike me lucky.

As busy as a bee.

Looking for new digs.

An apple a day, keeps the doctor away.

Shiver me timbers.

Dressed to the hilt.

Easy come, easy go.

As old, as the hills.

She's as pleased as punch.

They're eating me out of house and home.

You're in over your head.

She's a bit of a floozy.

Go suck a lemon.

If you can't stand the heat, get out of the kitchen.

As happy as Larry.

As poor as, a church mouse.

Hasta la vista, baby.

He's off his dial.

Just a basket case.

You're full of bright ideas.

That gives me the creeps.

Fits like a glove.

As pure as the driven snow.

You give me the pip.

Just a dumb Dora.

Don't take any wooden nickels.

As old as methuselah.

Little old biddy.

You take the cake.

Full as a tick.

He thinks he's the ducks guts.

As pretty, as a picture.

What a git.

You're just a ragamuffin.

Once, in a blue moon.

I'm plum tuckered out.

As the crow flies.

Whooping it up.

Flogging a dead horse.

Old fuddy-duddy.

Flying by the seat of his pants.

What the dickens.

That's fiddle sticks.

Ornery so and so.

Snug as a bug, in a rug.

As thick, as thieves.

That looks spiffy.

You're on your tod.

I'll give you a wallop.

Bless his heart.

Just the bee's knees.

What a nit wit.

Jiminy cricket, what is that?

He had me in stitches.

Your darn toot-in it is.

Is that ridgy-didge?

By Jove your right.

That's a fine kettle of fish.

That's using your old bean.

True-blue Aussie.

Wouldn't have the foggiest.

One for the birds.

He's too big for his britches.

Got your bobby socks on.

What a flapper.

As sober as a judge.

Merciful heavens, he didn't, did he?

Perish the thought.

Mind your manners, missy.

He's just a hooligan.

Little ankle biters.

Go put your galoshes on.

Look at those peepers.

I have a beef, with you.

She's a bit of a fruit loop.

He's come a cropper.

Bit light in the loafers.

As tough as, old boots.

Mad as a meat axe.

She's a bimbo.

What a yobbo.

Well, I'll be flabbergasted.

They're watching the idiot box.

You're as warm as toast.

Mind your P's and Q's.

Your cruising for a bruising.

They're chin wagging again.

Far out Brussel sprout.

On the warpath.

That's a snazzy top.

I never thought I'd see the day.

Heavens to Betsy.

He's just kicked the bucket.

Just a bit of a whipper snapper.

He is hammered.

Coming by snail-mail.

I'm just knackered.

As white as snow.

Bring home the bacon.

What a daft cow.

That was donkey's years, ago.

She fell arse over tit.

I've got the collywobbles.

Take a butcher's hook at that.

Let's skedaddle out of here.

Left me high and dry.

They are legless.

Hell, has no fury, like a woman scorned.

That's mint.

I'm back to square one.

Are you telling porkies again?

Let's have a knee's up.

I'm in the bad books.

Come hell or high water.

Plates of meat.

Getting all het-up.

On the wagon.

Bit of slap and tickle.

Read between the lines.

What a slapper.

He's just a hanger-on.

They're on the piss.

He was starkers.

Throw a spanner in the works.

It's all tickety-boo.

That's just bullshit.

Sock it to me.

That's a bloody whopper if I've ever heard one.

Not my cup of tea.

The back of beyond.

Back seat driver.

Little nest egg.

She'll badger him to death.

Never the twain shall meet.

Bald as a coot.

It's neither here, nor there.

Put a sock in it.

My old China.

Necessity is the mother of invention.

Stop banging on about it.

Barking up the wrong tree.

Waiting with, bated breath.

Be still my beating heart.

Nip it in the bud.

Rack your brains.

Putting the cart before the horse.

Been there, done that.

That put your nose out of joint.

He read me the riot act.

Beggars can't be choosers.

That's below the belt.

What a bludger.

Revenge is a dish, best served cold.

It's all bells and whistles.

You can bet your bottom dollar.

Big fish in a small pond.

The quick and the dead.

He's in a pickle.

Blast from the past.

Put on your thinking cap.

Gone to rack and ruin.

I'm in a quandary.

Blind leading the blind.

It's ten clicks that way.

Good things come in small packages.

That's my Sheila.

Walking at snail's pace.

He's just a loafer.

Let's go for a schooner.

Kneejerk reaction.

That's up the back of Bourke.

I'm going to bail out.

He's a true battler.

We're off to the big smoke.

Just beyond the black stump.

Bloody oath, mate.

Pull your horns in.

Don't let that blowie in.

Knock on wood.

Jump on the band wagon.

He just had a blue with the missus.

They're off bush bashing.

I couldn't give a continental.

Mind your own bizzo.

Just been in a bingle.

Put the billy on.

That's ace mate.

See you this arvo.

I'm chocka mate.

Push the boat out.

On the fiddle.

Keeping a stiff upper lip.

Not within cooee.

That's big bikkies.

She's in la-la land.

Lock stock and barrel.

Mad as a cut snake.

Prick up your ears.

Is that dinky-di?

As cunning as a dunny rat.

Fair suck of the sav. (Wonder, awe, disbelief)

Pigs arse, it is.

She'll be apples.

Look before you leap.

It never rains, when it pours.

That was point blank.

Keep that under your hat.

Mrs Lardy-dardy.

Like a moth to a flame.

Touch wood.

Scared the living daylights out of me.

Another lame duck.

He who laughs last, laughs longest.

Left in the lurch.

Up at sparrow's fart.

The cats got your tongue.

Green-eyed monster.

I haven't got a brass razoo.

A friend in need, is a friend indeed.

Lo and behold.

Where there's a will, there's a way.

Hard hearted.

Cheer up, it may never happen.

Lay it on with a trowel.

Okeydokey.

When everything's coming your way,
you're in the wrong lane.

If you can't beat'em, join'em.

God created the world, everything else is made in China.

Let's paint the town red.

No room to swing a cat.

It's not over till the fat lady sings.

Head over heels.

Getting a bit of shut eye.

Bit of a lick and a promise.

Less is more.

It's not rocket science.

Giving up the ghost.

A leopard never changes its spots.

O ye, of little faith.

Gone off half-cocked.

Just trust your gut.

Man, does not live on bread alone.

Alive and kicking.

The whole kit and caboodle.

In the red.

Let bygones be bygones.

Movers and shakers.

If wishes were horses, beggars would ride.

Every dog has its day.

As high as a kite.

On cloud nine.

Getting on my goat.

Hanky-panky.

Like it or lump it.

It's all doom and gloom.

Make no bones about it.

A kangaroo court.

How now, brown cow.

The graveyard shift.

Up there in her ivory tower.

The real McCoy.

Garlic makes a man, wink, stink, and drink.

My better half.

Bit of a rough diamond.

Give him a wide berth.

Chip off the old block.

Put your clod-hoppers on.

By hook or by crook.

A drop in the ocean.

Hung, drawn and quartered.

Caught, red handed.

Go the whole nine yards.

Take it with a pinch of salt.

To meet one's waterloo.

Mutton dressed as lamb.

Bun in the oven.

Wouldn't have a clue.

Cock-sure of yourself.

Joined at the hip.

There but for the grace of god, go I.

Eat humble pie.

You're getting my dander up.

Real motley crew.

Hair of the dog that bit you.

Call a spade a spade.

Going like the clappers.

Much of a muchness.

Every cloud, has a silver lining.

Let your hair down.

It was like a bolt from the blue.

Excuse my French.

The pen is, mightier than the sword.

Goody, goody gumdrops.

Hot off the press.

Drop-dead gorgeous.

He's done a runner.

Crocodile tears.

A double whammy.

Off his own bat.

Milk of human kindness.

Thinks he's gung-ho.

Nosy parker.

It's no laughing matter.

A feather in his cap.

Don't count your chickens, before they hatch.

Green eyed monster.

That's off the record.

Marry in haste, repent at leisure.

Is the pope a catholic?

Grind to a halt.

You'll get your just deserts.

What a crackpot.

Got his foot in the door.

Eat, drink, and be merry.

Cook the books.

Can't get a word in edgeways.

Half-hearted try.

On a wing and a prayer.

I'm just hunky-dory.

A woman needs a man, like a fish needs a bike.

More fool you.

Gone off half cocked.

As heavy as, lead.

A little bird told me.

What a load of cobblers.

Got my mojo back.

That's a death trap.

What a sorry sight.

Forewarned is forearmed.

That's a no brainer.

Make a pig's ear of it.

Cut to the chase.

We're getting down to tin tacks now.

Keep your pecker up.

Break a leg.

He'll cotton on to you.

A nod is as good as a wink.

It's a rust bucket.

He carries the weight of the world, on his shoulders.

As close as the grave.

In the doldrums.

Go the whole hog.

Blow your own trumpet.

Mumbo-jumbo.

That was a piece of cake.

He's a real grafter.

Handle her with kid gloves.

Got you over a barrel.

Fight fire with fire.

Got the world at his feet.

Panic stations.

As gentle as a lamb.

Dead ringer of his dad.

All above board.

Went down like a lead balloon.

P.D.Q. (Pretty, damn quick).

Has the penny dropped?

Calling it quits.

A picture's worth a thousand words.

In a pig's eye.

Got off on the wrong foot.

Frog in my throat.

An old clunker.

Pipe down you lot.

As calm as, a millpond.

That's daylight robbery.

Make my day.

You're getting on my wick.

Hoity-toity miss.

A fate worse than death.

Hold your horses.

It fell off the back of a truck.

Two timing, sod.

In the box seat.

All fingers and thumbs.

Fall from grace.

I'd love to be a fly on the wall.

She's a keeper.

Full of his own importance.

She's my broad.

Rule of thumb.

Got out of the wrong side of bed.

Double trouble.

What a heap.

He's chairman of the board. (Head of the household).

As easy as pie.

Run of the mill.

Fly off the handle.

As angry as hell.

Hasn't eaten a square meal in days.

That takes the cake.

What's up your nose.

Never trouble, trouble, till trouble, troubles, you.

The gift of the gab.

Useless as tits on a bull.

Come in sucker.

What a sweet little cherub.

In the wink of an eye.

Nutty as a fruit cake.

Silly old chook.

It's as clear as day.

As cool as a cucumber.

What an old bomb.

Mouth like a sewer.

That took forever.

As thick as, two short planks.

Lend me your ear.

Bull twang.

As blind as a bat.

Dumb as, a bag full of hammers.

He's double dipping.

What an oddball.

Chubby bubby.

That put the wind up him.

Pearls of wisdom.

Keep your eyes peeled.

Go over it, with a fine-tooth comb.

Your nit picking now.

Plumb tuckered out.

Your talking garbage now.

That's a tidy little sum.

You're driving me nuts.

I'm washing my hands of him.

As bold as brass.

Ground breaking news.

Bread, jam, and duck under the table.

That opened a can of worms.

As snug as a bug, in a rug.

Great balls of fire.

What a turd burger.

Bit wishy-washy.

Tomorrow is another day.

Get here pronto.

Easy as falling off a log.

A sandwich short of a picnic.

That's old hat.

I don't give a rat's arse.

Boring as bat shit.

Bald as a badger.

Spick and span.

As ugly as sin.

Spitting image, of you.

What a top bloke.

Eats like a bird.

You'll eat every morsel of that.

I'll bear that in mind.

Printed in the United States
By Bookmasters